ISBN: 9781763753259

First Edition

Wobbly Roo

Written & Illustrated by Pippa Bird

Amidst the gum trees,
Standing proud and tall.
Little Joey finds,
That his bounce is so small.

Born with one leg,
A little shorter than the other.
He learns to hop,
Guided by his mother.

His steps were uneven,
A stagger, a lurch.
But Little Joey's spirit,
Continued its search.

With each bound and leap,
Though often he tumbled.
In the whispers of the outback,
His courage rumbled.

All his friends cheered,
Their voices sang like a song.
As Little Joey practised,
Determined and strong.

With the clouds as his guide,
And the sun up above.
He hopped and he leaped,
His heart full of love.

Over rocks and through streams,
He found his own beat.
Learning that balance,
Means more than two feet.

In the rustle of bushes,
And the call of the cockatoo.
Little Joey jumped high,
A joyful little roo.

One day, as the rainbows
Arched over the skies.
He stood tall and proud,
With a twinkle in his eyes.

For in the heart of the bush,
amid nature's grand seat,
Little Joey had discovered
the strength of his feet.

For in every bound,
In every jubilant push.
The wobbly roo found his rhythm,
In the heart of the bush.

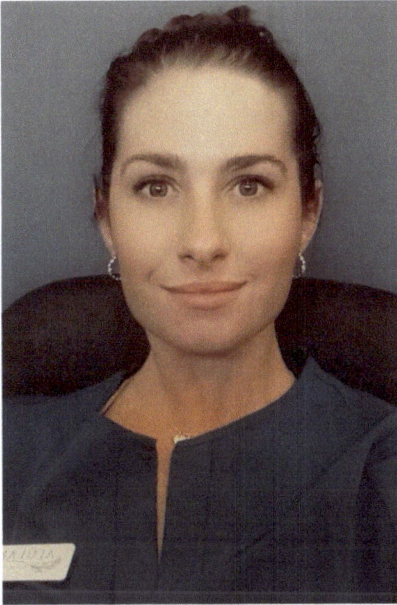

Calm Kangaroo

About the Author

Pippa Bird is a Mental Health Therapist in Private Practice in regional NSW. Pippa holds a Bachelor in Psychology, a Diploma in Counselling, and is currently undertaking a Postgraduate Degree in the field.

Pippa also holds a Diploma in Graphic Design, with a primary focus on illustration.

CALM KANGAROO is a backronym title for a children's mental well-being program. An initiative designed to educate children about mental health and foster a learning journey of emotional intelligence, resilience and cultivate an open mind through the power of reading well-being books, leading to the most important discussions and ideas.

The CALM KANGAROO program focuses on Curating, Advocating and Leading Mindfulness and its mission to Kindle Awareness, Nurture Growth, Amplify Resilience, and Orchestrate Open-minds.

ALULA BLU
COUNSELLING SERVICES

Calm Kangaroo is an Alula Blu Initiative

www.ingramcontent.com/pod-product-compliance
Lightning Source LLC
LaVergne TN
LVHW072112070426
835509LV00003B/132